MORE THAN A SURVIVOR

A DEVOTIONAL AND JOURNAL FOR THOSE HEALING FROM TRAUMA & ABUSE

LAINEY LA SHAY

More Than A Survivor
© 2023 by Lainey La Shay
ISBN: 979-8-9880822-0-0

Cover Design by Lainey La Shay.

Scriptures taken from the Holy Bible, New International Version®, NIV®. Copyright © 1973, 1978, 1984, 2011 by Biblica, Inc.™ Used by permission of Zondervan. All rights reserved worldwide. www.zondervan.com The "NIV" and "New International Version" are trademarks registered in the United States Patent and Trademark Office by Biblica, Inc.™

Images provided by Canva Pro.

ALL RIGHTS RESERVED
No part of this publication may be reproduced or transmitted, in any form, stored in a retrieval system, or transmitted in any form by any means—electronic, mechanical, photocopying, recording, or otherwise—without prior written permission of the author, except as provided by United States of America copyright law.

While the author has made every effort to provide accurate internet addresses and phone numbers at the time of publication, the author does not assume any responsibility for errors or for changes that occur after publication. Further, the author does not have any control over and does not assume any responsibility for third-party websites or their content.

SUBSCRIBE!
Subscribers get access to all the latest updates from Lainey about new releases, FREE bonus extras, and other behind-the-scenes access. Visit **www.laineylashay.com** to subscribe today.

⁂

For the women and men who have
faced the unimaginable.
I believe you.
I see you.
Let's heal from these things together.

⁂

Welcome!

Hello Dear Friend,

I never expected trauma or abuse to enter my life, and I know that you never thought it would be a part of yours. Yet here we are, you and I, standing at the beginning of a long journey called healing. It may look like a long, dry, and dusty desert stretching before you, but I want you to know that you don't have to make this journey alone.

While you may wonder how a loving God could let this happen, know that He is right here with you. He will carry you when you have no more strength and run out of willpower. He will hold and protect you when the nights get dark, and fear taunts you from the edges of your campfire. And He will rejoice with you for every step you take forward, learning something new about yourself and finding your strength.

You may have friends and family who long to come beside you and help you on this journey. Right now, you may want to put up walls, but please keep a back door open for those who want to love on you and show you that the world isn't made of darkness. Lay down your fear and pride and let them support you, whether it's someone to keep you company or to bring you a meal at the end of a trying day.

And, dear friend, I am here too, writing these words to you. Know that I am thanking God for you right now, and I am praying that you will heal, thrive, and know peace. I hope the words in the following devotions will shine some encouragement and hope into your week.

HOW TO USE THIS DEVOTIONAL

I know how hard it can be to concentrate on things right now and how challenging reading and writing can be when you are surviving trauma. These bite-sized devotions are here for you at your pace. Take your time, and feel free to read them in any order if one topic stands out to you more than another. But most of all, let it help heal your heart.

Within these pages, you'll find space to write or draw your thoughts and feelings if you choose. There are coloring pages for when you feel fidgety and need to focus and calm your racing mind. I've found that expressing myself in creative ways, on paper, can be life-giving; however, I understand if you aren't ready to do this. The space is here for you when you need it.

Remember, you are so loved. You are strong and courageous. And you are a **more than a survivor**. Though this healing journey will take time and bring a mix of hurt and joy, I promise you it does get better, and I know that you, like me, can make it through. Take my hand, and let's start on this journey together.

Light and Life,

Lainey

DAY ONE:
YOU ARE AMAZING

First things first: Has anyone told you how amazing you are today? Have you told yourself that?

I know that right now, you may not feel amazing. Chances are, you feel beaten up, bruised, confused, exhausted, and broken. You may even feel unloveable and worthless. Perhaps you've come out of a relationship where your value has been trampled time and again. You've started to believe lies that you're not enough. You might feel anger, rage, and grief. And you know what? It's totally OK to feel this way.

But even though you may feel these things, sometimes all at once, I want to remind you that you are amazing. Your trauma doesn't define you, my dear friend. It is something that happened to you and impacted you in significant ways, but it doesn't change the fact that you are wonderful. The world is a better place with you in it.

No matter what you are going through, what has happened, or what your past looks like, here are a few things you should know about yourself. If possible, you should say these out loud in front of a mirror and repeat them as often as possible to yourself.

- **You are amazing.**
- **You are strong.**
- **You are intelligent.**
- **You are brave.**
- **Your thoughts and feelings are valid.**

- **You are a survivor.**
- **You are an overcomer.**
- **You are beautiful.**
- **You are worthy.**
- **You are loved, cherished, and appreciated**

Do you believe those things about yourself? Maybe you did once, and your experience has rattled those beliefs.

Imagine a campfire or wood fireplace that has burned down until only embers remain. Even the tiniest of sparks is enough to reignite a blazing fire that gives off incredible warmth. We need to tend the fire, give it proper fuel, and prod it along sometimes to get it crackling again.

Even if your flames have gone out, I hope you'll try to rekindle them from the embers still simmering inside you. Continue to tell yourself that these things are true. I certainly believe that they are.

"Why?" you may ask.

Even if we haven't met face to face, I know some things about you. You haven't given up hope and haven't surrendered to your circumstances. You want to thrive.

And, friend, I believe you will.

PRAYER

Lord, sometimes it's hard to remember that You created me to be unique in all the world. My gifts, talents, passions, and personality are exactly as You intended them to be. You created me to be fierce, fabulous, and creative. You made me with strength, courage, and resilience and continue to give me hope. You have given me the power to bless others even in the middle of my pain. Remind me that even though I am hurting, I can still reach out a hand to others. It's a miracle and a mystery how doing so can help heal me too.

JOURNAL

In the space below, write or doodle some positive affirmations about yourself. What do you believe about yourself? What are your strengths? What brings you joy? What ignites the fire inside of you?

"

IT'S OK IF YOU FALL DOWN
AND LOSE YOUR SPARK.
JUST MAKE SURE THAT
WHEN YOU GET BACK UP,
YOU RISE AS THE WHOLE
DAMN FIRE.

COLETTE WERDEN

DAY TWO:
HAVE YOU EATEN TODAY?

Driving across the dusty desert in Arizona was the last place I expected to be that February morning. I never expected to be in an abusive marriage or that I would have to flee for my safety. But here I was, running for my life and praying my husband wouldn't find me.

Though no one knew where I was, a few friends and family had sent messages to check in and make sure I was okay. When they asked, "How are you?" I didn't know how to respond. My life had imploded, and I was operating at the most basic levels. Was I alive? Yes. Functioning? If you could call it that.

My phone rang somewhere along I-40, and my boss' voice came through the line. The first thing she asked me was, "Are you safe?"

Yes. At that moment, anyway.

Then she asked this: "Have you eaten today?"

Eaten? I blinked. I had forgotten to eat for three solid days.

Her following questions were, "Have you showered today? Did you brush your teeth?" These may sound like silly questions for one adult to ask another. But these things are easy to forget in moments of trauma and fear.

She stayed on the phone with me until I pulled over at the first restaurant I saw and got something to eat, then had me text her when I had accomplished the other basic tasks.

Those little things were huge for me in those first six weeks and for months after. Simple routines, good food, and self-care made me feel infinitely better, cleared my head, and kept my body healthy.

If you've experienced trauma and are struggling to make it through the day, it's all too easy to forget to take care of your basic needs. If we continue that pattern long enough, our bodies will wear out and break down. We will find ourselves getting sick, exhausted, and facing medical issues. That's the last thing you need on top of all you've already faced, my friend.

Try to make healthy decisions for yourself every day, especially concerning meals. Sometimes a pizza or a pint of Ben & Jerry's seems the easy answer. But your brain and body need good nutrients to function and make critical decisions. Try to cook at home, even if it's something basic, and get a good balance of protein, carbs, healthy fats, and vegetables. Some nights, exercising a little culinary creativity might just boost your spirits.

PRAYER

Lord, help me to take care of my body as I heal from this trauma. Give me the stamina to make it through things one at a time, and give me strategies to help me succeed. You've created my body to be strong and resilient. Help me recognize the importance of fueling my body in positive ways.

JOURNAL

In the space below, write or draw the answers to the following questions. How do you feel when you eat enough of the right things? How do you feel when you don't? List a few ways you can keep fueling your body positively, even on tough days.

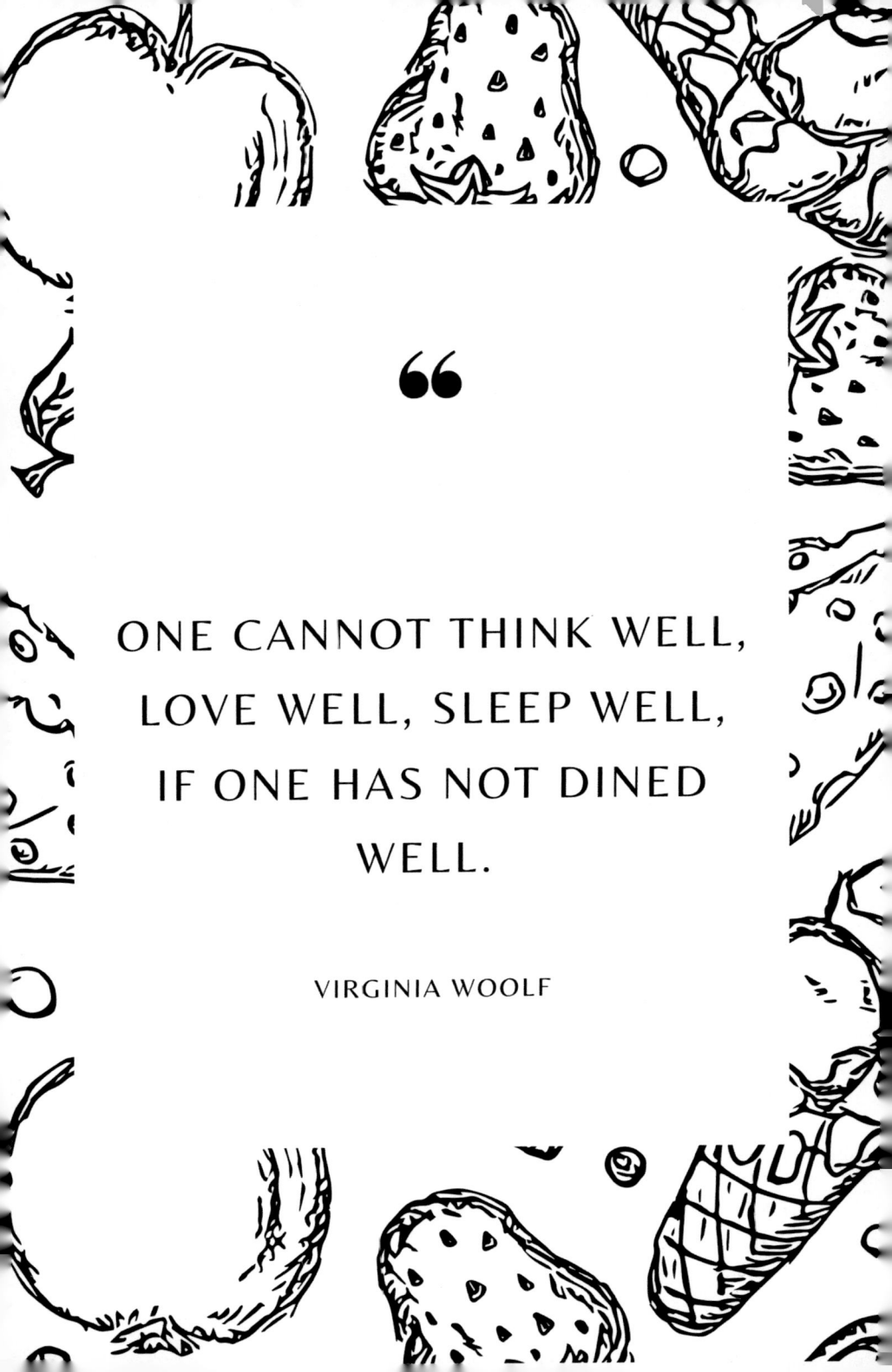

"

ONE CANNOT THINK WELL,
LOVE WELL, SLEEP WELL,
IF ONE HAS NOT DINED
WELL.

VIRGINIA WOOLF

DAY THREE:
IT'S NOT ALL IN YOUR HEAD

The white-capped waves crashed against the California shore two weeks after I fled home. No one except the friends who were helping me knew where I was.

And if we're being honest, I didn't know where I was either. After fifteen years of abuse, I had been trained to question my reality. And so a big chunk of my brain wondered if this was all in my head.

Had all of this been a dream I'd wake up from at any moment? Was I in a coma somewhere, lost in the deep pools of my imagination? Or had I just flat-out gone insane and was imagining myself on the warm, sandy beaches of California rather than in the snow-packed Midwest?

You may not be in the same situation that caused me to question my reality. However, the trauma that you've faced can definitely cause some doubts. No matter how you or I frame it, the truth is that none of this is in your head. Your whole body and brain know the fear and trauma you have experienced (and sometimes, it will keep throwing you back there to those moments).

It is easy to wonder how this could have happened to you or why it happened in the first place. We often obsess over the string of events that led to that crisis point. It's hard to imagine that something this tragic could take place. It's stranger than fiction sometimes. When you envisioned how your life should look, you never imagined this.

Know that I see your pain, friend. And it's OK to feel the way that you do about it. Your feelings are a hundred percent real and valid. You have every right to feel this way after what you've experienced. Be kind to yourself when you feel like reality is spinning, and know it's not all in your head.

PRAYER

Lord, this situation that I'm in is crazy-making. Some days I don't know right side up from upside down, real from imaginary, lies from truth. The Bible says if we ask Your Holy Spirit for wisdom and knowledge, You will give it in abundance. So I ask You to please provide me with wisdom and knowledge. Please show me what is true about my situation and about myself. This reality where I find myself is difficult, and the hurt runs deep. Please help me to find the courage to face it, to acknowledge that my experience and feelings are valid, and to accept help to allow my body and mind to heal.

JOURNAL

One of the things I've found most helpful is documenting things that happen during my day. I can return to those notes when I start to doubt if they happened or forget details. Doing a bit of journaling can also be a great way to organize thoughts when they feel jumbled in your head. These entries don't have to be long and can be as detailed as you like. Today, you might want to practice documenting the day's events and journaling your thoughts and feelings. Take a few moments to jot down or draw what you know to be true about yourself and your situation in the space below.

66

IF ANY OF YOU LACKS
WISDOM, LET HIM ASK OF
GOD, WHO GIVES TO ALL
LIBERALLY AND WITHOUT
REPROACH, AND IT WILL
BE GIVEN TO HIM.

JAMES 1:5

DAY FOUR:
SIT WITH YOUR THOUGHTS

After six weeks in hiding, my husband took his own life. This added a whole new dimension to the trauma I had already experienced, heaping even more on top of what was already there.

While I acknowledged the reality of what had happened, I didn't want to think about it. I hated feeling the sickening waves of grief and confusion that pummeled me day and night. So I kept myself busy at all waking hours — working, organizing, selling my home, running laps, watching movies, you name it.

A few weeks later, I punched a wall for the first time in my life. A few days after that, I kicked a toolbox. What hurt worse than my bruised toes and knuckles, however, was knowing that this was not me. How had I changed from being a gentle spirit to one with serious rage issues?My counselor figured out in five minutes flat that I had been burying my thoughts and emotions. I was creating an explosive situation by refusing to acknowledge them as they surfaced. "You're acting like a volcano," she told me. "You're bottling everything up under the surface where you can't see it. The more you put there, the more pressure it creates. Eventually, you will bust a seam, and all that emotional lava will come erupting to the surface. And those explosions are violent."

But I didn't want to feel those things ever again. And I'm guessing you don't want to think about them either.

"Your mind and body are going to experience these thoughts and feelings one way or another," my counselor told me. "You might as well experience them in a healthy way."

She proceeded to tell me about a Jewish tradition called *sitting shiva*. When a close family member or friend dies, mourners sit for seven days and do nothing but process their grief. They don't shave, shower, wash clothes, or work. They do nothing but sit with their thoughts and feelings. This allows a healthy way to process what has happened before they resume their lives.

Now, you and I both know that life doesn't often allow us to sit for a week and process our emotions. The world keeps turning, annoying as that can be some days. Healing from trauma also takes more than a week to do. But if we are intentional about sitting with those thoughts as they rise to the surface each day, we can make some progress.

So when those thoughts and feelings come up today, tomorrow, and next week, think through them. Feel through them. Cry if you must. Scream into a pillow. Whatever it takes. But acknowledge them when they knock on the door, so they don't end up blowing the door, and you, down.

PRAYER

Lord, I need your help. If I could forget this hurt ever happened, I would do so in a heartbeat. I don't want to think about it anymore, and I'm tired of getting knocked down when the emotions hit. Sometimes they feel as if they're breaking me even more than I already am. Remind me that You can make beauty out of ashes. Give me comfort. Please help me find the courage to sit with these thoughts and think through them. Show me how taking the time to do this can help and heal me.

JOURNAL

Take some time to write or draw answers to the following questions in the space below.

- What things and activities do you do to avoid thinking about your trauma? How do you avoid feeling emotions when they surface?
- In what ways can you learn to sit with your feelings and thoughts? How can you give yourself the time and grace to do so?
- What are you feeling today? What thoughts are dancing at the edge of your mind?

"

IF YOUR HEART IS A
VOLCANO, HOW SHALL
YOU EXPECT FLOWERS TO
BLOOM?

KHALIL GIBRAN

DAY FIVE:
YOU DON'T DESERVE THIS

Car lights danced across the popcorn ceiling in my apartment as the minutes passed with the steadiness of the dripping faucet. Light from the hall kept the darkness from suffocating me. Sleep was elusive as my mind replayed what had happened. Where did it all go wrong? What could I have done differently? What if I had seen the signs sooner?

How often do you lie awake at night, exhausted and unable to stop thinking about the trauma you experienced? How often do you replay it and the events leading up to it?

How often do you think:
- If only I'd done something different...
- If only I'd been somewhere else...

- If I had been a better wife/husband/partner...
- If I'd worn this...
- If I'd said that...

The "what-if" and "if-only" lists can go on forever if we let it. We kick ourselves for not knowing better or doing something different, even if we never saw this coming.

I want to tell you something right now, and I want you to read this out loud. Ready?

THERE IS NOTHING YOU DID TO DESERVE THIS OR CAUSE THIS. IT ISN'T YOUR FAULT.

No matter what happened, know that you tried as hard as possible and did your best with the information and skills you had at the time.

I understand and see the pain you feel and know the questions you ask yourself and the blame you put on yourself for what happened. Remember, my friend, you are not to blame for what happened, and you are not responsible for the actions and words of others. You are beautiful and worthy and did not deserve any of this.

This isn't easy to do, but try and make a conscious choice to stop asking yourself those questions. You and I can only go back to change things if someone invents a time machine. So what good does it do to torture ourselves by asking ourselves what we would change when there's no way to do so? Instead, think of things you hope for or that bring you joy. Repeat a favorite encouraging quote or Bible verse. (My favorite is below.) Occupy your mind by listening to a sleep story that provides positive images and helps you rest.

PRAYER

Lord, you know how often I lie awake at night wondering what I could have done differently. You know how often I beat myself up for not knowing better or for having seen the warning signs. You know how often I lie awake, still full of fear from what happened, wondering if it's all over, bracing myself for it to happen again, and wondering when. Please calm and quiet my mind and give me rest. Help me to know that I did nothing to cause this or deserve it.

JOURNAL

Write down the phrase in bold above. *"There is nothing you did to deserve this or cause this. It isn't your fault."* Decorate it however you would like. Write it as many times as you would like.

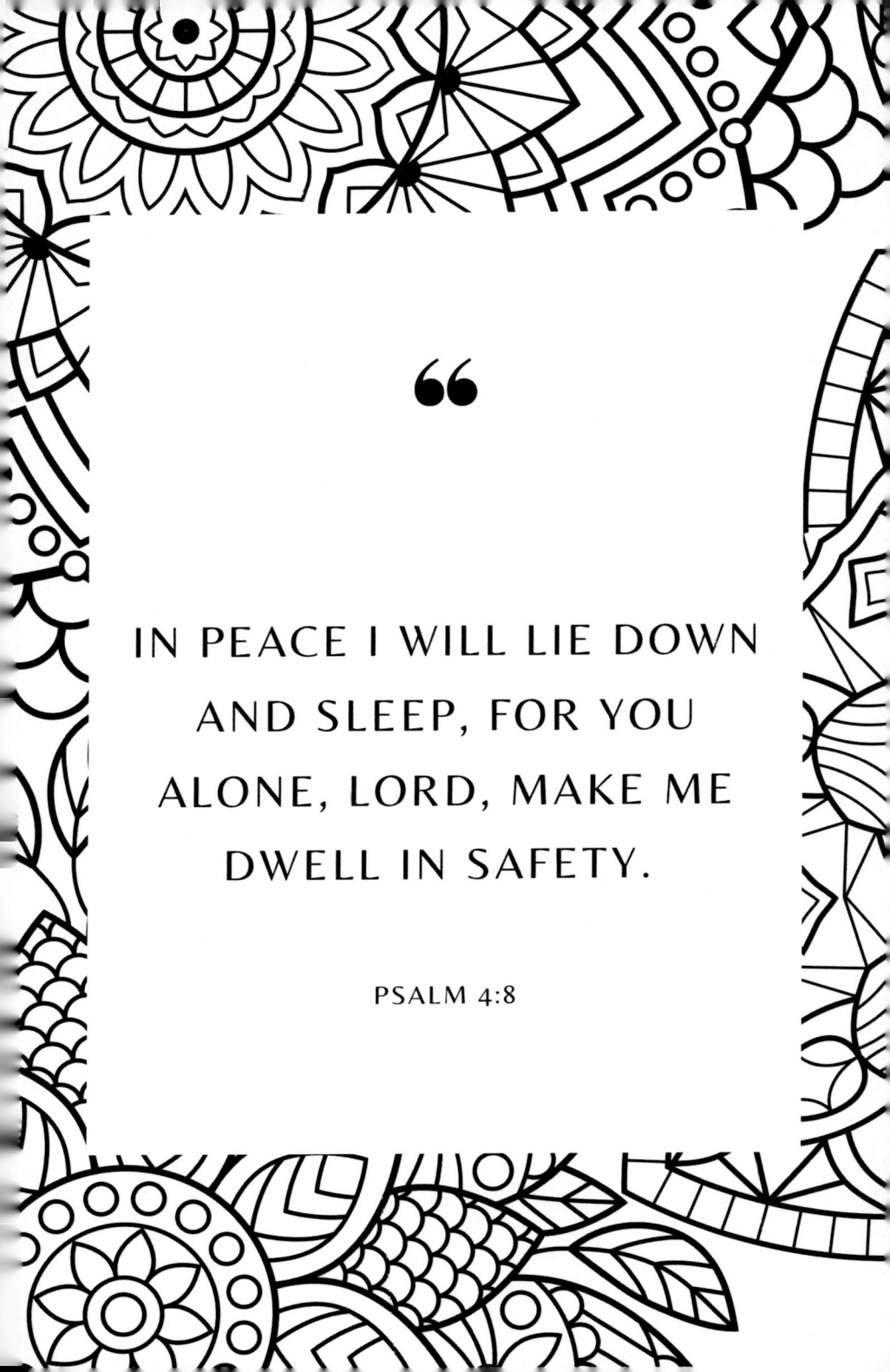

"

IN PEACE I WILL LIE DOWN
AND SLEEP, FOR YOU
ALONE, LORD, MAKE ME
DWELL IN SAFETY.

PSALM 4:8

DAY SIX:
SETTING BOUNDARIES

Have you ever had to say no to something or someone? I know I sure have. It's hard to do, isn't it? We get so anxious and afraid that laying down healthy boundaries will make things worse. But in the end, doesn't it usually end up bringing you peace?

Imagine we're standing in a beautiful city on the seashore that has walls and levees to prevent the ocean from sweeping in and flooding the streets. If those boundaries between the sea and the town were removed, the lives of people in it would be washed away — sometimes gradually, sometimes in the blink of an eye. Having those levees and seawalls in place allows the town to grow and thrive and for the people inside it to live in peace.

One of the things I've had to learn to do after walking through trauma is to set healthy boundaries with myself and others.

Boundaries are important to have on a good day but are essential when one has been through the storms of trauma like you and I have.

To prevent damage and drowning, we need to make sure that we're putting those boundaries up when and where we need to.

Sometimes this means:
- Turning off the TV
- Taking a step back from social media
- Stopping unhealthy coping mechanisms or habits
- Telling people "no" when it stretches you too thin
- Setting limits with others
- Blocking calls and walking away from people who are toxic and abusive.

All of these can be so difficult to do and enforce. Setting boundaries can bring anxiety and fear with it. Sometimes we are tempted to return to the familiar, even if it is hurting our bodies, minds, and hearts. But doing the difficult task of setting boundaries can lay the groundwork for healing.

PRAYER

Lord, it can be difficult to set healthy boundaries and say "no." Please help me know who I need to set boundaries with, how to set those boundaries, and the courage to enforce them. Please help me to remember that boundaries can be healthy and life-giving and that I deserve safe relationships. Give me the strength to keep moving forward and not return to people and relationships that are toxic or crazy-making. Show me the peace and freedom I can have by setting these needed boundaries.

JOURNAL

What do healthy boundaries look like for you? Are there boundaries that you need to set with yourself? Are there others with whom you need to create some healthy boundaries? And, are there certain people with whom you need to part ways? Use the space below to write or draw your thoughts

"

SOMETIMES YOU HAVE TO
MAKE A DECISION THAT
WILL BREAK YOUR HEART
BUT HEAL YOUR SOUL.

TRENT SHELTON

DAY SEVEN:
WHAT HEALING LOOKS LIKE

Most people think that healing is a straight line on the chart. As time goes on, healing increases. Right? Let me tell you a secret. Healing looks more like a toddler has colored swirls and squiggles all over your freshly painted wall. And sometimes, it's just as maddening.

Healing is a journey and requires us to show up every day and put one foot in front of the other. To be clear, sometimes showing up means that you showered. Giving yourself rest on the days when you are exhausted to do otherwise is productive. On days when you feel stronger, you might accomplish other things, such as starting a new project, organizing your house, or picking up a new hobby. Don't define your day by how many items you checked off your to-do list. Do what you can do each day and start fresh the next. One impossible thing at a time.

Most of all, friend, be gentle with yourself. Show yourself kindness, and give yourself grace.

You inspire me. Did you know that? Even though you may not notice how far you've come, you are making progress. It takes a lot to recover from trauma. You are doing your best every day, and I can see the progress that you are making.

Keep going, my friend. I won't promise you it will be easy, but I will tell you that it does get better. And if anyone can make it and come out of this thriving, I know it's you.

PRAYER

Lord, healing is messy business. How I wish it weren't that way! My head feels like it's full of a bunch of broken crayons and nonsense scribbles on the walls. Help me to remember that broken crayons still color and that you can create something beautiful from my broken pieces. Remind me that there is hope and healing, even if I don't see how it's possible right now. Remind me that You are there with me and that I'm never alone.

JOURNAL

Draw or describe in the space below what you think your healing journey has looked like so far.

66

BROKEN CRAYONS
STILL COLOR.

DAVID WEAVER

RESOURCES

National Domestic Violence Hotline
- (800) 799-SAFE (7233)
- thehotline.org

National Suicide Prevention Lifeline
- (800) 273-8255
- suicidepreventionlifeline.org

National Sexual Assault Hotline:
- (800) 656-HOPE (4673)

Find a Counselor
- locator.apa.org
- https://christiancounselors.network/

EMDR Therapists for Trauma
- emdria.org

Moving Ahead: A Financial Empowerment Resource
- https://allstatefoundation.org/what-we-do/end-domestic-violence/resources/

FURTHER READING

- *The Body Keeps the Score* by Bessel van der Kolk

- *Getting Past Your Past* by Francine Shapiro, Ph.D.

- *What Happened to You?* by Oprah Winfrey and Dr. Bruce D. Perry

- *Good Boundaries and Goodbyes* by Lysa Terkeurst

- *Called to Peace: A Survivor's Guide to Finding Peace and Healing After Domestic Abuse* by Joy Forrest

- *Is It My Fault? Hope and Healing for Those Suffering Domestic Violence* by Justin and Lindsey Holcomb.

- *Domestic Abuse: Help for the Sufferer* by Darby Strickland

- *The Emotionally Destructive Marriage* by Leslie Vernick

- *Shame Interrupted: How God Lifts the Pain of Worthlessness and Rejection* by Edward Welch.

IMPORTANT PHONE NUMBERS

My Counselor
Name: _____
Phone Number: _____
Email: _____

Police
Name: _____
Phone Number: _____

Doctor
Name: _____
Phone Number: _____

A Friend or Relative I Trust and Can Talk To:
Name: _____
Phone Number: _____

A Friend or Relative I Trust and Can Talk To:
Name: _____
Phone Number: _____

A Friend or Relative I Trust and Can Talk To:
Name: _____
Phone Number: _____

IMPORTANT PHONE NUMBERS

Other:
Name: _____
Phone Number: _____
Email: _____

Other:
Name: _____
Phone Number: _____

Other:
Name: _____
Phone Number: _____

Other:
Name: _____
Phone Number: _____

Other:
Name: _____
Phone Number: _____

Other:
Name: _____
Phone Number: _____

"

MY WISH FOR YOU IS THAT
YOU CONTINUE. CONTINUE TO
BE WHO AND HOW YOU ARE,
TO ASTONISH A MEAN WORLD
WITH YOUR ACTS OF
KINDNESS. CONTINUE TO
ALLOW HUMOR TO LIGHTEN
THE BURDEN OF YOUR
TENDER HEART.

MAYA ANGELOU

DOCUMENTATION

My friend, I understand that abuse can be ongoing and can happen post-separation. This is a heartbreaking reality, and I am grieved that you are walking through it. Below is space for you to document instances of ongoing or post-separation abuse. Though it is difficult to do, it is critical to document these things in case you ever need to present them to a police officer or court of law. Take courage and reach out for help if you need it. You are not alone.

DOCUMENTATION

My friend, I understand that abuse can be ongoing and can happen post-separation. This is a heartbreaking reality, and I am grieved that you are walking through it. Below is space for you to document instances of ongoing or post-separation abuse. Though it is difficult to do, it is critical to document these things in case you ever need to present them to a police officer or court of law. Take courage and reach out for help if you need it. You are not alone.

DOCUMENTATION

DOCUMENTATION

DOCUMENTATION

DOCUMENTATION

DOCUMENTATION

DOCUMENTATION

DOCUMENTATION

DOCUMENTATION

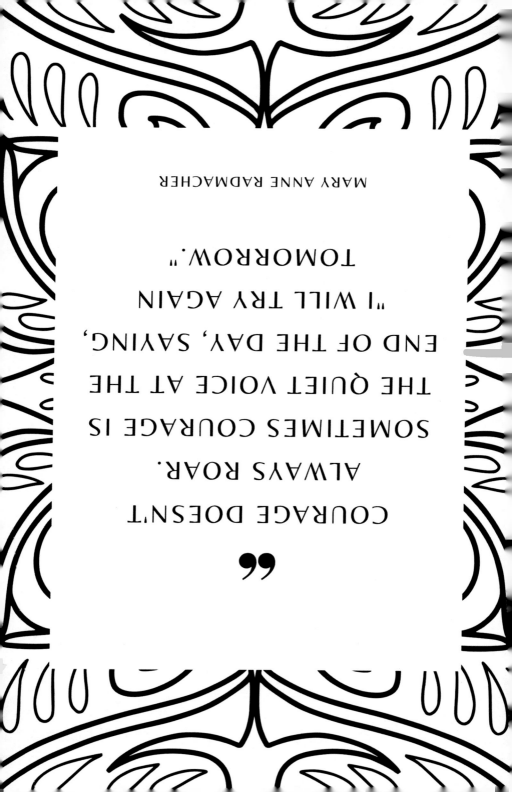

> COURAGE DOESN'T ALWAYS ROAR. SOMETIMES COURAGE IS THE QUIET VOICE AT THE END OF THE DAY, SAYING, "I WILL TRY AGAIN TOMORROW."

MARY ANNE RADMACHER

NOTES & REMINDERS

NOTES & REMINDERS

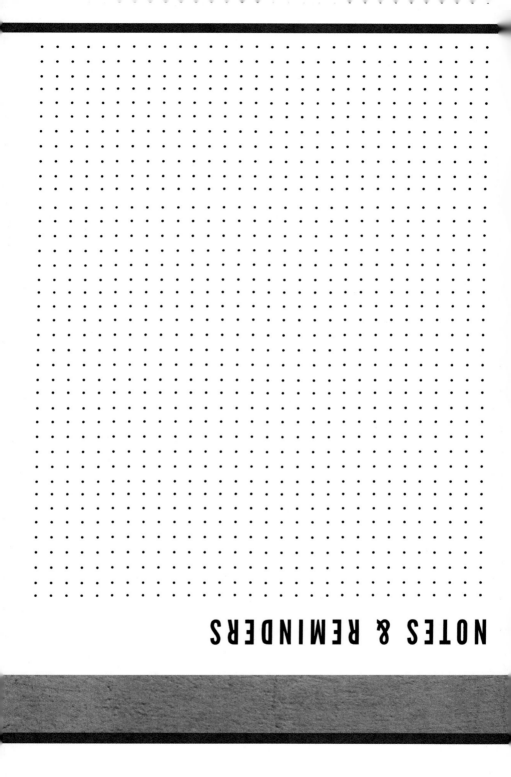

NOTES & REMINDERS

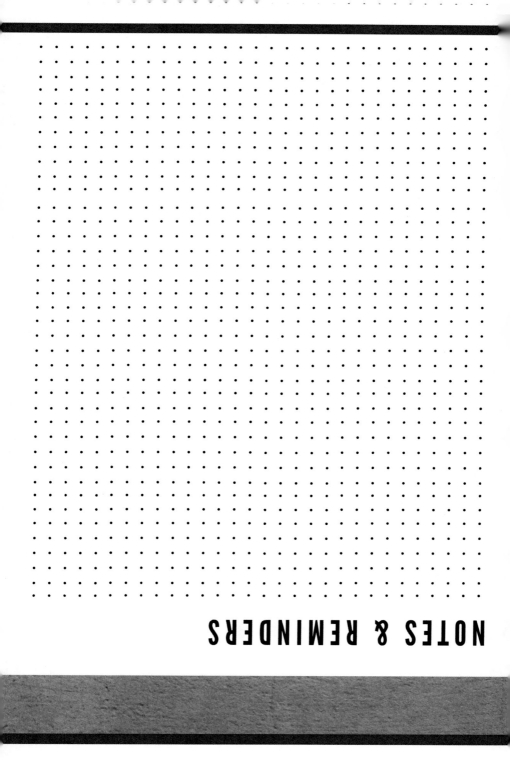

NOTES & REMINDERS

NOTES & REMINDERS

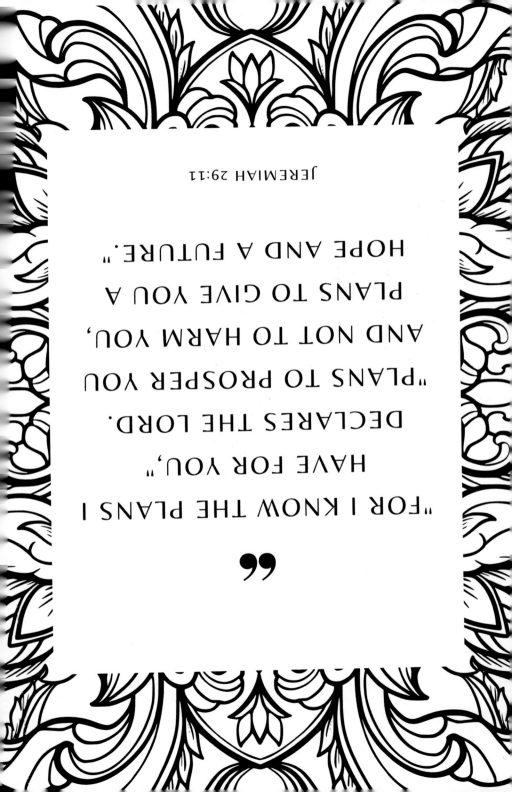

> "For I know the plans I have for you," declares the Lord. "Plans to prosper you and not to harm you, plans to give you a hope and a future."

JEREMIAH 29:11

NOTES & REMINDERS

Made in the USA
Las Vegas, NV
29 September 2023